Beads

Your best source for beads is a bead shop or a craft or needlework shop that carries beads. There are also many mail-order and internet sources. Because there are so many different beads, do not worry about trying to get the exact bead listed for each project and feel free to make your own variations and creations!

Seed beads come in several sizes and even different shapes, although they are usually round and resemble little seeds. Common sizes are 11/0 and 6/0. The larger the number, the smaller the bead. Sometimes seed beads are referred to as rochailles.

Bugle beads are tubes that are available in many different lengths.

I have used the term 'decorative beads' to refer to beads other than seed or bugles. They are great accents and attention getters on tassels, fringes and pouch straps. Use them as the centerpiece for some of your creations!

Thread & Needle

To sew beads on fabric, use a thin, sturdy beading thread such as Nymo which is available in many colors. Generally medium or darker colors are less noticeable than white. The thinner weights of Nymo are easier to thread in the small eyes of beading needles. Thin weights also allow you to pass through size 11/0 seed beads more than once which is necessary on the fringed edgings.

Sometimes the edges of bugle beads are sharp enough to cut through thread. If you use bugles on pouch straps, I recommend using a very fine nylon coated wire to prevent your strap from coming apart. Soft Touch™ is one brand that comes in .010 diameter and drapes nicely for necklace type straps.

Use a long size 12, 13 or smaller beading needle when stringing beads for fringe. Shorter needles are suitable for sewing beads directly onto fabric. The larger the beading needle number, the smaller the size.

Stitching Beads to Fabric

Anchor the thread by making several small, short stitches on top of each other at an inconspicuous place on the fabric. Tug the thread to be sure it is secure before adding beads. Snip off the loose tail close to the anchor stitches.

Outline Stitch - Stitch down one or two beads at a time or couch a strand of beads by stitching between every other bead.

When stitch[ing] beading, you needed.

If you are working on a bottle, you should leave at least a 6" tail to weave back and forth through existing beadwork to secure the thread. Test by tugging on the last few beads you added to ensure they cannot be moved. When you change directions, loop thread around a single bead and take the needle back into the beading. Trim the tail close to the beading.

Start a new thread by weaving it back and forth several times through existing bead paths. When the thread is secure, continue your beading.

Bead Tassels

Anchor the thread and add on a base bead of your choice. Continue adding beads to make your first strand. At the end of the strand, fter adding the last seed bead, pass the needle back through the rest of the beads and into the fabric. Stitch once through the fabric, then bring the needle back out through the base bead and make another strand.

Continue adding several strands of varying lengths to make the tassel. If the base bead becomes too full of thread to pass the needle through, start new strands just below it. You will need to make one final pass through the base bead to anchor the thread in the fabric and finish the tassel.

Image Transfer

There are several methods available to transfer images to fabric. Each comes with a complete set of instructions. If you do not have access to a computer with an inkjet printer, transfer color copies with liquid transfer medium. Remember to reverse the image when making a copy or printing so the image will be correct when applied to the fabric. The following products give good results.

Plaid Picture This liquid transfer medium.

Photo Effects Iron-on Transfer Paper for inkjet printers.

Photo Effects Iron-on Transfer Paper for color copies.

Clasp Top Pouches

Create little pouches with the look of Victorian fancy work. All you need are a gilded purse clasp, scraps of elegant fabrics and a few embroidery stitches. Add a beaded fringe to finish your heirloom treasure.

Assemble Frame - Use metal purse frames as indicated to fit patterns or adjust the pattern by altering the top above the dotted line to fit a different frame.

1. After you have decorated the pouch front, place right side on right side of back piece and sew together below the dots. Trim seams, clip curves and turn right side out.

2. If the pouch does not have a lining, turn the top edge under twice in a narrow hem and baste.

3. If pouch has a lining, sew right sides together, trim seams and clip curves but do not turn. Insert lining in pouch and turn remaining raw edges of both to inside along seam allowance and baste.

4. Open the purse frame and stitch the pouch to the holes in the frame one side at a time with doubled sewing thread. Align the hinge of the frame to the dot on the pouch pattern. Manipulate the fabric to fit within the frame. It is not an exact science. Since you are working by hand, you will be able to adjust as you stitch.

5. To cover the stitching threads on the frame, add beads at each hole using a beading thread and needle.

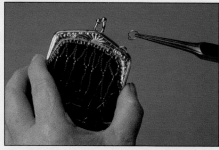

6. Attach chains or bead strings to loops on frame with jumprings or split jumprings for extra security.

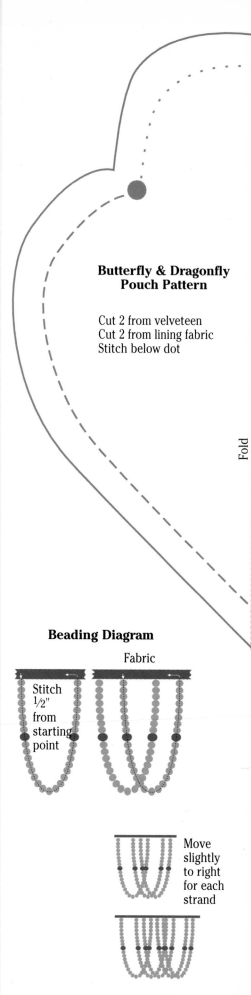

Butterfly & Dragonfly Pouch Pattern

Cut 2 from velveteen
Cut 2 from lining fabric
Stitch below dot

Fold

Beading Diagram

Fabric

Stitch ½" from starting point

Move slightly to right for each strand

Dragonfly & Butterfly Pouch

MATERIALS:
Plum velveteen and lining fabric • Lacis
Purse Frame silver #LS67 • 2" wide blue ombré ribbon
• Organza ribbon • HeatnBond Lite iron-on adhesive • Kreinik #8
metallic green braid • Kreinik #1 silver Japan Thread • Kreinik
Balger metallic rainbow cord • Beading thread and needle • Sewing
thread and needle • 2 split jumprings

BEADS: Two ⅝" green bugle beads • 7mm green glass bead •
12mm x 10mm oval green bead • Two 6/0 orange silver lined
seed • Three 6/0 chartreuse silver lined seed • 2 packages
of 11/0 violet spark silver lined seed • 1 package of 8/0
golden plum inside rainbow seed • 1 package of 5/0
amethyst silver lined bugle

INSTRUCTIONS: Cut velveteen and lining pieces
as directed on pattern.

Dragonfly - Trace wing patterns on paper side
of iron-on adhesive. Fuse to the back of
organza ribbon and cut out each wing piece.
Fuse wings to the pouch front. Couch a
strand of rainbow cord with rainbow cord
around the outer edge of all wing components. Feather stitch veining on the wings.
Blanket stitch shadow below wings. With
green metallic braid, straight stitch antennae.
Stitch the beads in place as shown to form the
head, thorax and body. Add orange eyes at the
end of the head.

Butterfly - Trace butterfly wings on paper side of
iron-on adhesive and fuse to back of ombré ribbon.
Cut wings and fuse to pouch back. Blanket stitch
around wings with #1 silver Japan thread. Make head and
body from chenille yarn. Make a French knot head. Use ½"
long straight stitches to start the body, then go back and
wrap more chenille around the stitches for dimension. Sew
seed beads around wing borders, and use decorative beads for
embellishing the wings.

  Assemble pouch and lining. Attach to clasp top. Stitch an 11/0 seed
bead over each hole.

  Bead the fringe as shown on the diagram.

  Make a simple 39" strap by alternately stringing bugle and 8/0 plum
beads on wire secured to split rings. Attach split rings to loops on clasp top.

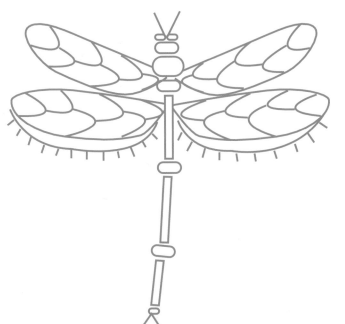

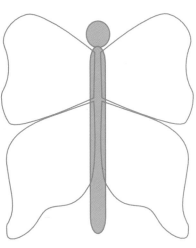

Embellish a butterfly on the
back side of the pouch.

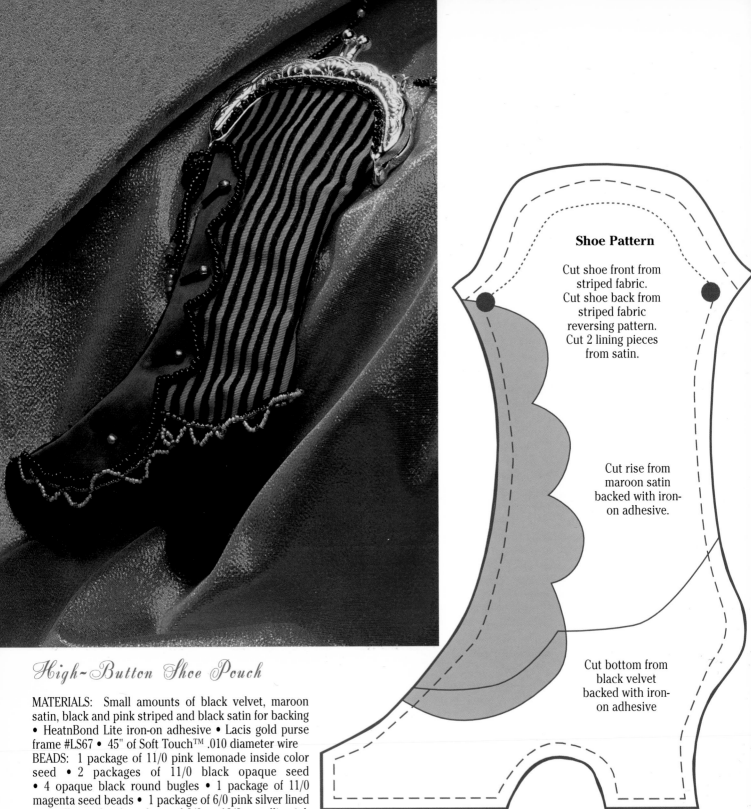

High~Button Shoe Pouch

Shoe Pattern

Cut shoe front from striped fabric. Cut shoe back from striped fabric reversing pattern. Cut 2 lining pieces from satin.

Cut rise from maroon satin backed with iron-on adhesive.

Cut bottom from black velvet backed with iron-on adhesive

MATERIALS: Small amounts of black velvet, maroon satin, black and pink striped and black satin for backing • HeatnBond Lite iron-on adhesive • Lacis gold purse frame #LS67 • 45" of Soft Touch™ .010 diameter wire

BEADS: 1 package of 11/0 pink lemonade inside color seed • 2 packages of 11/0 black opaque seed • 4 opaque black round bugles • 1 package of 11/0 magenta seed beads • 1 package of 6/0 pink silver lined rochaille seed • 1 package of 9/0 or 10/0 metallic pink seed • Four 3mm gold beads

INSTRUCTIONS: Cut pattern pieces as directed. Fuse black velvet to right side of shoe front first and maroon satin second overlapping the velvet a bit.

Outline stitch 11/0 black beads along edge of satin and 11/0 magenta beads along edge of velvet.

Stitch 4 buttons in place using one black bugle and 3mm gold bead for each.

Sew a simple looped fringe of 11/0 pink beads to magenta beads. Pass needle through an existing magenta bead, add four 11/0 pink, 11/0 magenta, four pink and go through sixth magenta bead to right. Repeat along entire magenta bead row.

With right sides together, stitch shoe front to back below dots at sides and bottom. Clip curves and turn right side out. Finish top edges with narrow hems and stitch to purse frame. Stitch 11/0 black beads over each hole of frame.

At top of shoe make a simple tie by securing beading thread and stringing black seeds for 2" to 3" ending with 4 metallic pink beads and a single black bead. Loop around the black and go back through the strand. Secure to fabric and make an identical strand. Secure to fabric with blind stitches. Tie the 2 strands together with a soft bow.

Make a 39" strap by stringing Soft Touch wire with 11/0 black seeds and occasional 6/0 pink and metallic pink beads. Attach to frame.

Bee Pouch

MATERIALS: Pink handkerchief with crocheted edge • Lacis silver purse frame #LS69 • 5" square of fusible interfacing • Green, purple, dark pink and blue silk ribbon • Silk ribbon embroidery needle • 45" of Soft Touch™ .010 diameter wire

BEADS: 11/0 spearmint transparent rainbow seed • 11/0 pink lemonade inside color seed • Assortment of beads for strap

BEE MATERIALS: Black felt • Yellow 4mm silk embroidery ribbon • 28 gauge beading wire • Kreinik silver or gold #1 Japan thread or confetti cord • Kreinik #8 black braid • 5mm or 6mm round black bead

INSTRUCTIONS: Fold handkerchief in half and cut. Fold one half in half again and cut. Set the ½ handkerchief piece aside. Turn the raw edges under on the 2 remaining pieces and press.

Cut interfacing to reinforce the embroidery area of the front panel and trim to fit within seam allowances. Iron on wrong side of front. Do simple silk-ribbon embroidered flowers using French knots, lazy daisy and straight stitches.

Bee - Cut 2 black felt ovals and trim one ⅛" smaller all around. Loosely gather the edge of the larger oval and stuff the smaller oval into it. Stitch larger oval to pouch front. Make 2 or 3 stripes by stitching across the oval with yellow silk ribbon. Trace 4 wing shapes on HeatnBond Lite. Fuse to organza and remove paper. Twist 4 lengths of wire into wing shapes with 1½" tails, position on adhesive side of organza and place another layer of organza on top. Fuse the wire between the organza layers. Trim wing shapes leaving a slight overhang of fabric. Whip stitch around wing edges with Japan thread or confetti cord. Work feather stitches on each wing for veining. Push the wire tails into the bee body and stitch to back of fabric. Sew the black bead on for head. Stitch antennae by adding a french knot at the end of 2 black braid straight stitches.

With right sides together, stitch front and back of pouch between dots at sides. Clip to top dots and turn right side out. Top stitch the bottom edges of the pouch closed along crocheted edge. Stitch beads along the stitching line and to the crocheted trim.

Fold and trim the the top corners to fit the purse frame turning under raw edges. Stitch fabric to frame.

Add a simple looped bead fringe to frame. Bring beading thread out through first hole on left. String on 12 pink beads and stitch into fourth hole from left. Bring thread back out through third hole from left, add 12 beads, go in seventh hole from left. Repeat the process until the entire top is loop fringed. Some holes will be used for starting and ending different loops.

Whip stitch the sides of the pouch closed. Stitch loops of beads along seams by stringing 10 beads, stitch to fabric so they form an arch, bring needle back up through last bead and add nine more beads, stitch and repeat.

Secure one end of the wire to the purse frame and add assorted beads in any pattern for 19½". Reverse the bead pattern for the second half of the strap and secure to other side of purse frame.

Bee Pouch Patterns

Cut 2 from handkerchief

Fold

Cut one from fusible interfacing

Bee Pattern

Cut 4 wings with 2 layers each from organza.

Spider Web Pouch

MATERIALS: 5" x 6" pieces of velvet for each side of pouch • Satin lining fabric • 5" square of fusible interfacing • Lacis silver purse frame #LS 58 • Spider charm • Kreinik #1 and #5 silver Japan thread • 45" of Soft Touch™ .010 diameter wire

BEADS: Two 4mm silver lined bugle • 11/0 American blue opaque frost seed • 11/0 diamond silver lined seed • 8/0 golden plum inside rainbow

INSTRUCTIONS: Cut 2 pattern pieces each from velvet and satin fabric. Transfer web design to interfacing. Cut out circle and fuse to wrong side of pouch front. Couch #5 silver Japan thread with #1 silver Japan thread to work the web design on front of velvet. Place the spokes first then radiate the spiral out from the center. Stitch the spider charm in place with silver thread.

With right sides together, stitch lining front to back below dots using ¼" seam allowance. Clip curves and turn right side out. Fold in top edges along seam allowance and finish with narrow hems. Stitch each side to purse frame.

Stitch a solid row of 8/0 plum beads in the seam line. Go back and add bead extensions at the ends of the spider web spokes extending to seam beads in the following pattern: one plum, one silver bugle, one silver seed, back through bugle, one plum and stitch through seam bead.

Stitch a blue bead over each of the holes on the frame back and a plum bead over each of the holes in the frame front. Add a beaded fringe to the front starting at the center and working to the right. Go back to the center and repeat the steps working to the left to complete fringe.

Secure one end of the wire to the purse frame and add blue, silver and plum beads in any pattern for 19½". Reverse the bead pattern for the second half of the strap and secure to other side of purse frame.

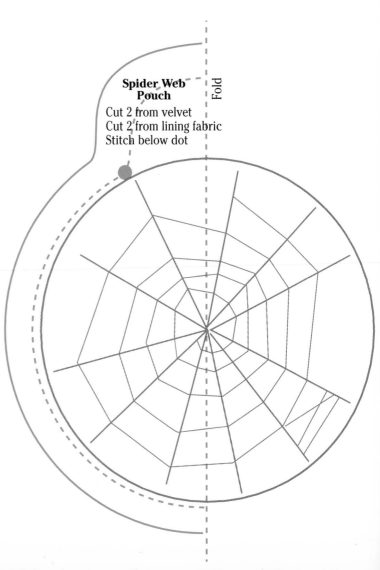

Center

Spider Web Pouch
Cut 2 from velvet
Cut 2 from lining fabric
Stitch below dot

Fold

Edge of pouch

Spider Web Fringe

Ribbon Pouch

MATERIALS: 12" of 2" wide ombré satin ribbon • Lacis gold purse frame #LS64 • 45" of Soft Touch™ .010 diameter wire

BEADS: 11/0 purple inside color seed • 8/0 paradise blue inside rainbow seed • 8/0 violet blue inside rainbow seed • Size 2 silver lined bugle • Size 5 cobalt blue silver lined bugle • Lavender rice pearls • 2 gold filigree beads • Two 7/0 rochailles • Kreinik #8 metallic purple braid

INSTRUCTIONS: Finish ribbon ends with narrow hems. Fold ribbon in half and whip stitch sides closed with metallic purple braid. Fold bottom corners to center, and tack halfway up with an 8/0 blue bead. Fold the corners back down and tack in place with beads. Add a beaded tassel to the point at the bottom.

Stitch the top of the ribbon to the frame folding and manipulating to fit. Cover each hole with an 8/0 violet bead. Add beaded fringe following the diagram.

Secure one end of wire to the purse frame. Add one filigree and one 7/0 rochaille and then assorted beads in any pattern for 19½". Reverse the bead pattern for the second half of the strap and secure to other side of purse frame.

Ribbon Fringe

Center

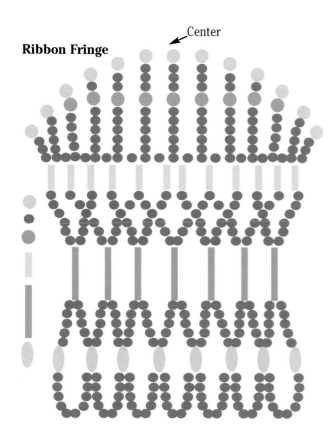

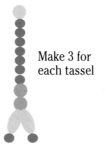

Make 3 for
each tassel

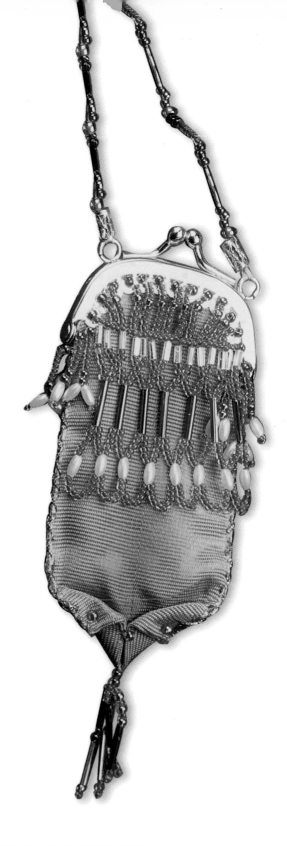

Tip:
Many ribbons have wired edges. Simply pull out the wires and discard them. If you want to use a sheer ribbon for a pouch, add a lining for extra durability.

Sensational Sachets

Nothing is more romantic than a sweetly scented sachet. Sachets made of rich fabrics and embellished with beads are true pleasures to possess and to share with the special people in your life.

Sachet Assembly

1. Decorate sachet front following pattern directions. Cut out sachet front, fold in half. Fold backing fabric in half and place the folded sachet front on backing fabric. Trace around the sachet front adding 1" to the center of the bag for overlap. Cut 2 pieces.

2. Turn under ¼" along each center edge of the back pieces and stitch.

3. Align front and back pieces with right sides together and overlap the finished edges of the backs. Stitch around edges and turn right side out.

4. Whip stitch the center seam of the sachet about halfway. Fill sachet using a paper funnel or plastic bag. Do no try to stuff the sachet as you would a pillow, just fill out the shape. Finish stitching center seam.

Tip: Use a fine textured dried filling such as lavender buds. Do not use oily fillings that may stain the fabric. When filling is no longer fragrant, simply take out stitching and refill.

Sachet Backs

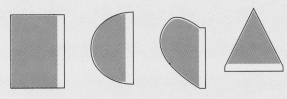

Fold sachet top in half. Place on doubled backing fabric and trace around shape adding 1".

Whip Stitch

Dragonfly Sachet

SACHET MATERIALS: 8" x 7" piece of magenta satin • 5" x 6" piece of plum velveteen • HeatnBond Lite iron-on adhesive • Organza for back • Size 5 lavender perle cotton thread • Embroidery needle

BEADS: Mauve bugle beads • 10/0 pink metallic seed • 11/0 violet spark silver lined seed

DRAGONFLY MATERIALS: Organza ribbon • HeatnBond Lite iron-on adhesive • Kreinik #8 metallic green braid • Kreinik Balger metallic rainbow cord

BEADS: Two ⅝" green bugle • 7mm green • 12mm x 10mm oval green • 8mm x 6mm teardrop • Two 6/0 orange silver lined seed • Three 6/0 chartreuse silver lined seed

INSTRUCTIONS: Trace oval pattern on paper side of iron-on adhesive. Fuse to wrong side of velveteen and cut out oval. Fuse to center of sachet top.

Dragonfly - Trace wing patterns on paper side of iron-on adhesive, fuse to the back of organza ribbon and cut out each wing piece. Fuse wings to the velveteen oval. Couch a strand of rainbow cord with rainbow cord around the outer edge of all wing components. Feather stitch veining on the wings. Blanket stitch shadow below wings. With green metallic braid, straight stitch legs and antennae. Stitch the beads in place as shown for the head, thorax and body. Add orange eyes at the end of the head.

Sachet Embellishment - Work a closed blanket stitch around the edge of the oval using lavender perle cotton thread. At the end of each point, sew a metallic pink bead. Sew front of sachet to back and turn right side out. Top stitch ¼" from outer edge. Work bead fringe around edge of sachet starting at one corner. String violet, mauve bugle, violet, bugle and violet. Stitch to sachet edge ¼" to ⅜" from anchor point. Bring thread back up through last violet and continue the sequence around the edge. Fill and close sachet.

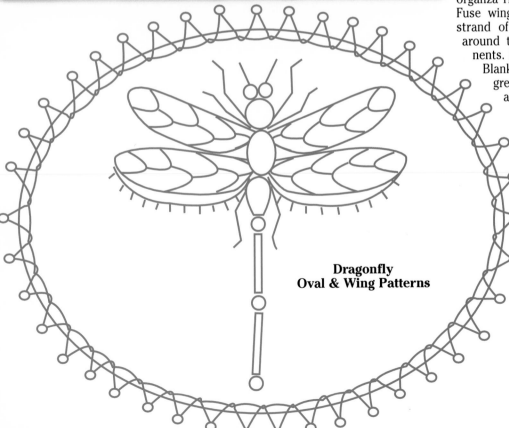

**Dragonfly
Oval & Wing Patterns**

Porcupine & Rose Sachet

MATERIALS: 9" square of purple velveteen • 18" x 9" piece of lavender organza • HeatnBond Lite iron-on adhesive • 1 yard of 1½" wide purple ombré wire edge ribbon • Metal leaf motif • Silver thread

BEADS: Short silver bugle beads • 11/0 purple silver lined seed • 11/0 purple blue lined seed • 84 silver 6mm beads • 84 blue black ½" bugle

INSTRUCTIONS: Top stitch oval shape on velveteen and cut away center. Cut edges and turn under. Cut iron-on adhesive and use it to fuse the velveteen to lavender organza.

Sew bugle beads all over the velveteen being careful not to extend into the seam allowances. Anchor thread to back of fabric, come up and add a bugle and purple seed. Loop thread around the seed bead, then go back through the bugle and fabric. Move needle about ¼", come up through fabric and add another bugle/seed unit. Repeat to cover the top of the velveteen.

Stitch top to back and turn right side out.

Work bead border around the edge of the sachet. Come up through fabric, add a 6mm silver bead, ½" blue-black bugle and 11/0 blue lined seed. Pass needle back through bugle, silver bead and fabric. Move needle a short distance and repeat.

Tack the metal leaf motifs to sachet by using silver thread to make several short stitches across the stems.

Make gathered rose and stitch on sachet as shown. Fill and close sachet.

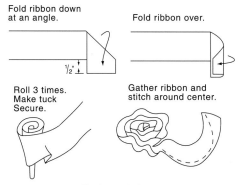

Gathered Rose

Fold down one edge of ribbon at 45° angle to extend ½". Fold again as shown. Roll ribbon 3 times, secure with thread. Make a ½" tuck. Stitch. Measure half of remaining ribbon and gather stitch along the long edge to the halfway mark. Pull gathers tight and wrap around center. Secure ruffled ribbon to center of flower with stitches. Gather stitch along remaining edge of ribbon. Slant stitches across width of ribbon at end. Pull stitches tight as possible. Wrap ribbon around previous ruffles and secure with stitches.

Lattice Sachet

MATERIALS: 6" square of lavender organza • Satin or silk for back • 2 yards of narrow velvet ribbon • Small white pearls • 11/0 purple seed beads

INSTRUCTIONS: Arrange strips of ribbon in a criss-cross pattern on the organza. Stitch each ribbon intersection to the organza by bringing the needle up through both layers of ribbon, add a pearl and one 11/0 purple seed bead, loop around the seed bead and go back through pearl, ribbon layers and organza. Take another stitch to anchor. Continue to next intersection and repeat.

Sew top to back, turn, fill and close.

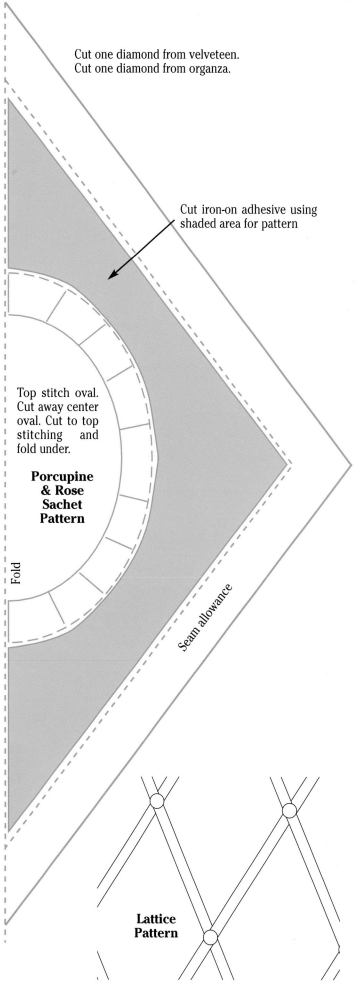

Cut one diamond from velveteen.
Cut one diamond from organza.

Cut iron-on adhesive using shaded area for pattern

Top stitch oval. Cut away center oval. Cut to top stitching and fold under.

Porcupine & Rose Sachet Pattern

Fold

Seam allowance

Lattice Pattern

Spiral Sachet

MATERIALS: 6" magenta organza circle for top (complete first step before cutting circle to size) • Satin or silk for back • Tissue paper • Kreinik #8 metallic pink braid • Embroidery needle • Embroidery hoop

BEADS: Small white pearls • Lavender metallic, magenta silver lined and pink silver lined 11/0 seed • 8/0 pink inside color seed • Mauve or pink bugle bead

INSTRUCTIONS: Trace the spiral pattern on tissue paper. Stretch the organza on top of the tissue in embroidery hoop. Work the spiral pattern in a simple blanket stitch using pink metallic braid and sew a lavender metallic seed bead at the end of each stitch.

Remove fabric from hoop and carefully tear away any remaining tissue paper. Trim to 6" circle.

Stitch top to back and turn right side out. Stitch bugle beads around the outer edge.

Between each bugle, sew mini tassels. Add a loop for hanging the sachet in place of one tassel by stringing 2" to 3" of 11/0 magenta beads above the pearl, passing needle back through the pearl and anchoring thread in fabric.

Mini tassel - Pass needle through existing bugle, add pearl, 8/0 pink, 5 magenta seeds. Pass needle back through the seeds, 8/0 pink bead and pearl. Take a stitch in the fabric and go back through the pearl and 8/0 bead. Repeat sequence to make second and third magenta strands. For the fourth strand, use three 11/0 pink seeds.

Fill and close sachet.

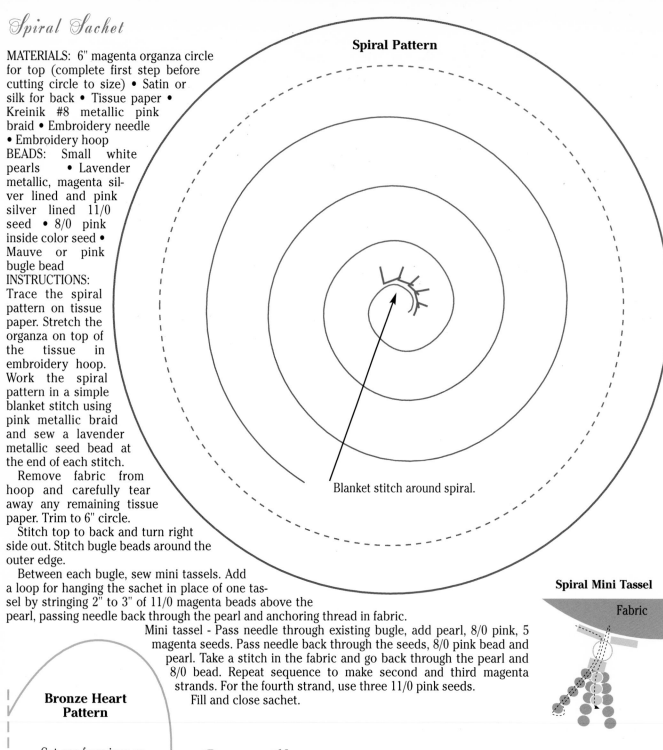

Spiral Pattern

Blanket stitch around spiral.

Spiral Mini Tassel

Fabric

Bronze Heart Pattern

Cut one from iron-on adhesive.
Cut one from lamé.

Fold

Bronze Heart

MATERIALS: 7" square of green metallic organza • Brown printed velvet for edging and back • 5" square of bronze lamé • HeatnBond Lite iron-on adhesive • Kreinik #8 metallic bronze braid • Embroidery needle

BEADS: 11/0 metallic copper seed • 11/0 champagne silver lined seed • 8/0 bronze iris 2 cut

INSTRUCTIONS: Transfer heart pattern to paper side of iron-on adhesive. Fuse to wrong side of bronze lamé and cut out heart. Fuse heart to center of organza.

Feather stitch around edge of heart and sew a copper seed bead at the end of each stitch.

Stitch bead loops on heart by bringing needle up through fabric, stringing on 6 champagne, copper bugle, 6 champagne and going back down through fabric next to the first bead. Move needle a short distance, bring back up through fabric and repeat.

Sew 1¼" wide strips of velvet around edges of organza to frame it. Sew top to back and turn right side out. Top stitch where velvet and organza connect to complete the frame. Stitch radiating strands of champagne beads ending with a copper bugle at each corner of the organza.

Fill and close the sachet.

Bee Sachet

MATERIALS: 9" square of shimmery white organza • 9" x 12" purple embossed imitation suede cloth for heart appliqué and back • HeatnBond Lite iron-on adhesive • Yellow, variegated green and variegated magenta 4mm silk embroidery ribbon • Embroidery needle • Embroidery hoop • Silk ribbon embroidery needle
BEADS: 8/0 fuchsia inside color • 11 mint Ceylon • 11/0 lilac Ceylon • Two packages of 11/0 snowflake Ceylon • 11/0 cotton candy Ceylon
BEE MATERIALS: Black felt • Yellow 4mm silk embroidery ribbon • 28 gauge beading wire • Kreinik silver or gold #1 Japan thread or confetti cord • Kreinik #8 black braid • 5mm or 6mm round black bead
INSTRUCTIONS: Transfer heart pattern to iron-on adhesive. Fuse to wrong side of purple cloth and cut out heart. Mark diamond pattern outline on organza and fuse heart to center. Stretch organza in embroidery hoop and work feather stitches around heart with green ribbon. Make single and stacked lazy daisy stitches at ends of feather stitching for blossoms. Sew two or three 8/0 fuchsia beads in center of each blossom.

Bee - Cut 2 black felt ovals and trim one ⅛" smaller all around. Loosely gather the edge of the larger oval and stuff the smaller oval into it. Stitch larger oval on organza. Make 2 or 3 stripes by stitching across the oval with yellow silk ribbon. Trace 4 wing shapes on HeatnBond Lite. Fuse to organza and remove paper. Twist 4 lengths of wire into wing shapes with 1½" tails, position on adhesive side of organza and place another layer of organza on top. Fuse the wire between the organza layers. Trim wing shapes leaving a slight overhang of fabric. Whip stitch around wing edges with Japan thread or confetti cord. Work feather stitches on each wing for veining. Push the wire tails into the bee body and stitch to back of fabric. Sew the black bead on for head. Stitch antennae by adding a french knot at the end of 2 black braid straight stitches.

Sew top to back and turn right side out.

Stitch bead fringe around the edges. Make each fringe section from 3 loops of beads as follows: Outer loop - 3 white, pink, 6 white, lilac, 5 white, pink and 3 white. Middle loop - 3 white, pink, 5 white, lilac, 4 white, pink, 3 white. Inner loop - 3 white, pink, 2 white, lilac, 2 white, pink and 3 white. At corners, use fewer white beads in inner loop and more white beads in outer loop. Between each loop group, make a dangle of 2 white, pink, 7 mint and go back through pink and white beads.

Fill and close sachet.

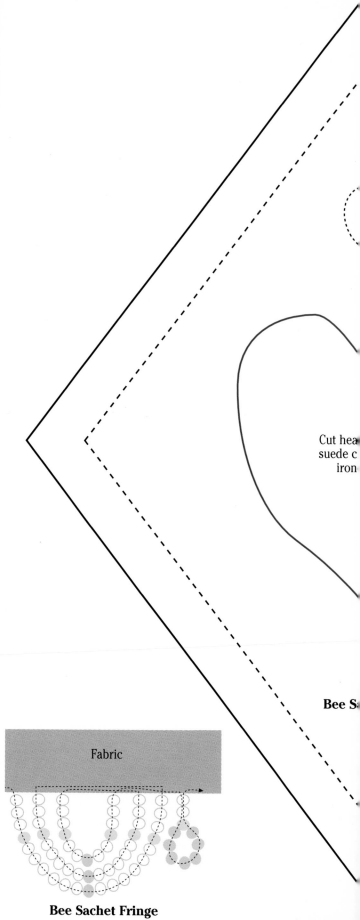

Fabric

Bee Sachet Fringe

Cut hea
suede c
iron

Bee S

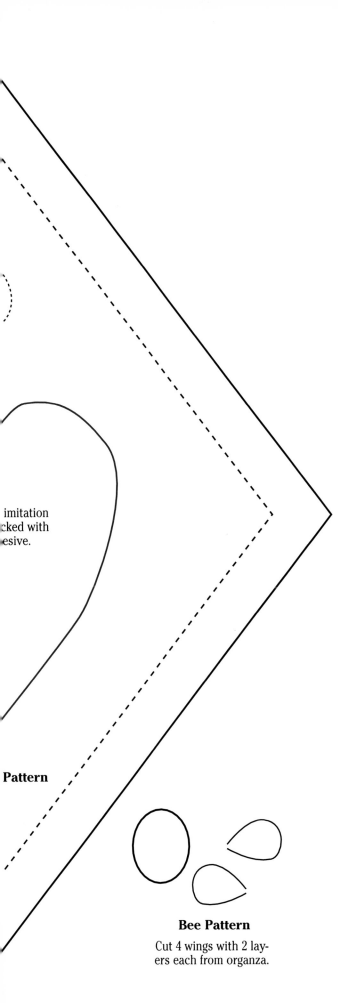

imitation
cked with
esive.

Pattern

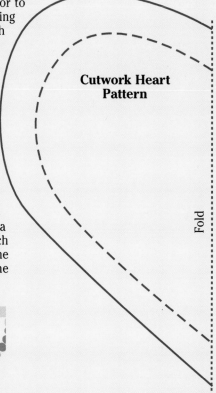

Bee Pattern

Cut 4 wings with 2 lay-
ers each from organza.

Cutwork
Velvet Heart

MATERIALS: 5" square of lavender organza • Magenta organza for back
• 4" square of blue velvet • HeatnBond Lite iron-on adhesive • Craft
knife • Rubber Stampede ornate heart decorative foam stamp •
Acrylic craft paint, any color • 18" length of ¼" silk ribbon for bow
BEADS: 6/0 cornflower silver lined • 6/0 diamond silver lined
• 11/0 diamond silver lined • 11/0 electric blue silver lined
INSTRUCTIONS: Cut heart from lavender organza. Stamp heart image
on paper side of iron-on adhesive with acrylic paint. Let dry. Fuse image
to wrong side of velvet. Carefully cut out the image using a very sharp
craft knife. Iron the cut image on the lavender organza heart.
   Sew front to back and turn right side out.
   Work bead fringe around edge as follows:
Round 1: Anchor a 6/0 diamond bead to fabric.
Add five 11/0 diamonds, blue, five 11/0
diamonds, 6/0 diamond. Anchor to
fabric about ½" from starting
point. Come back up through
last 6/0 diamond, add five
11/0 diamonds and repeat
around entire edge.
Round 2: Anchor cornflower
bead midway between 2 diamond and add 5 blue, 11/0
diamond, 5 blue and corn-
flower. Intertwine the blue
strands behind the first
strand of clear beads in
front of the second strand
and repeat. Anchor each
cornflower bead to fabric.
   Fill and close sachet. Make a
2" loop from ribbon and stitch
to the top of the heart. Tie the
remaining ribbon around the
loop in a bow.

**Cutwork Heart
Pattern**

Fold

Fabric

**Cutwork Heart
Fringe**

Velvet Cutwork

Make intricate looking cutwork... it's easier than you imagine. Rubber stamps are the secret!

1. Transfer pattern onto paper side of iron-on adhesive.

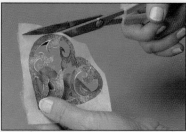

2. Trim close to the image.

3. Iron the adhesive on back of velvet.

4. Cut out velvet.

5. Iron velvet on fabric.

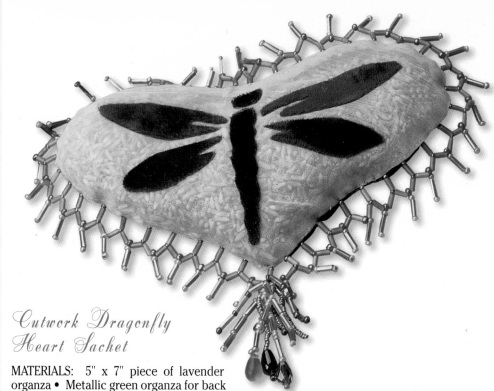

Cutwork Dragonfly Heart Sachet

MATERIALS: 5" x 7" piece of lavender organza • Metallic green organza for back • 3" x 5" piece of blue velvet • HeatnBond Lite iron-on adhesive • Craft knife • Plaid Stamp Decor dragonfly foam stamp • Acrylic craft paint, any color • 4" of narrow silk ribbon

BEADS: Frosted blue-gray bugle • Assorted decorative beads for tassel • 11/0 bluegrass Ceylon • 11/0 blueberry opaque luster

INSTRUCTIONS: Stamp dragonfly image on paper side of iron-on adhesive with acrylic paint. Let dry. Fuse image to wrong side of velvet. Carefully cut out the image using a very sharp craft knife. Iron the cut velvet pieces on the lavender organza heart.

Sew backing on sachet.

Work bead fringe around edge as follows:

Anchor beading thread to fabric. Add blueberry, bugle, blueberry, bugle, blueberry, bluegrass, bugle and bluegrass. Pass thread back through bugle, bluegrass and blueberry. Add bugle, blueberry, bugle, blueberry and anchor to fabric about ⅜" from starting point. Bring needle back through last blueberry, bugle, blueberry, add bugle, blueberry, bluegrass, bugle, bluegrass, loop, and continue around entire edge of heart.

Add a bead tassel at the point of the heart by making several strands of assorted bugle, seed and decorative beads.

Fill and close sachet. Make a loop from the ribbon and stitch to the top of the heart.

Fabric

Dragonfly Heart Fringe

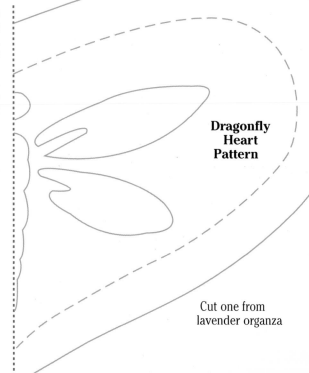

Dragonfly Heart Pattern

Cut one from lavender organza

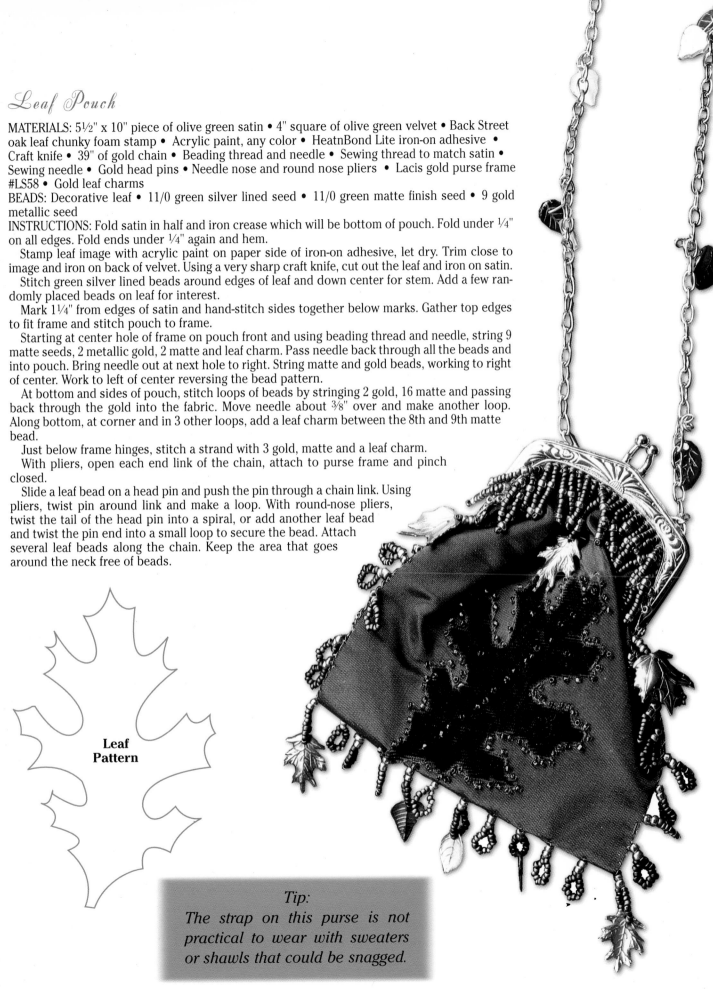

Leaf Pouch

MATERIALS: 5½" x 10" piece of olive green satin • 4" square of olive green velvet • Back Street oak leaf chunky foam stamp • Acrylic paint, any color • HeatnBond Lite iron-on adhesive • Craft knife • 39" of gold chain • Beading thread and needle • Sewing thread to match satin • Sewing needle • Gold head pins • Needle nose and round nose pliers • Lacis gold purse frame #LS58 • Gold leaf charms

BEADS: Decorative leaf • 11/0 green silver lined seed • 11/0 green matte finish seed • 9 gold metallic seed

INSTRUCTIONS: Fold satin in half and iron crease which will be bottom of pouch. Fold under ¼" on all edges. Fold ends under ¼" again and hem.

Stamp leaf image with acrylic paint on paper side of iron-on adhesive, let dry. Trim close to image and iron on back of velvet. Using a very sharp craft knife, cut out the leaf and iron on satin.

Stitch green silver lined beads around edges of leaf and down center for stem. Add a few randomly placed beads on leaf for interest.

Mark 1¼" from edges of satin and hand-stitch sides together below marks. Gather top edges to fit frame and stitch pouch to frame.

Starting at center hole of frame on pouch front and using beading thread and needle, string 9 matte seeds, 2 metallic gold, 2 matte and leaf charm. Pass needle back through all the beads and into pouch. Bring needle out at next hole to right. String matte and gold beads, working to right of center. Work to left of center reversing the bead pattern.

At bottom and sides of pouch, stitch loops of beads by stringing 2 gold, 16 matte and passing back through the gold into the fabric. Move needle about ⅜" over and make another loop. Along bottom, at corner and in 3 other loops, add a leaf charm between the 8th and 9th matte bead.

Just below frame hinges, stitch a strand with 3 gold, matte and a leaf charm.

With pliers, open each end link of the chain, attach to purse frame and pinch closed.

Slide a leaf bead on a head pin and push the pin through a chain link. Using pliers, twist pin around link and make a loop. With round-nose pliers, twist the tail of the head pin into a spiral, or add another leaf bead and twist the pin end into a small loop to secure the bead. Attach several leaf beads along the chain. Keep the area that goes around the neck free of beads.

Leaf Pattern

Tip:
The strap on this purse is not practical to wear with sweaters or shawls that could be snagged.

Ribbon Pouches & Sachets

Luxurious ribbon… beautiful designs… elaborate beaded fringe… this combination creates pouches that are tiny works of needle art.

1. Fold a strip of ribbon in half.

2. Turn top edges under and stitch

3. Whipstitch sides to finish.

4. Sew beads to bottom folded edge for fringe.

Porcupine Heart Pouch

MATERIALS: 7" of 2½" burgundy velvet ribbon with gold imprinting (remove wire from the edges if applicable) • Antique gold or bronze lamé • HeatnBond Lite iron-on adhesive • 45" of Soft Touch™ .010 diameter wire • Beading thread and needle • Sewing thread and needle

BEADS: 4mm gold beads • Gold bugle beads • 8/0 metallic gold seed • 10/0 red transparent rainbow seed • 7mm gold bead • 11/0 metallic gold seed • Size 2 Christmas red silver lined round bugle

INSTRUCTIONS: Fold ribbon in half and turn under top edges. Whip stitch to finish.

Mark fold which will be the bottom edge of pouch.

Trace heart shape on paper side of iron-on adhesive. Fuse to wrong side of lamé and cut out heart. Fuse heart to front of pouch.

Stitch red seeds around the heart just inside the edges. To make the porcupine filling, come up with the needle, string red bugle and gold seed, pass needle back through bugle and fabric. Pull snug to make the beads stand up vertically. Move needle a short distance, come up through fabric and repeat.

At the bottom of pouch, fold the square corners up into the pouch to make an angle and stitch to secure.

Starting in the center, work bead fringe around the bottom using red and gold bugles, 4mm and seed beads.

Strap - Secure wire at top corner of pouch. String a 7mm gold, seed and bugle beads for approximately 2½". Add a 7mm gold and repeat bugles and seeds. At the third 7mm gold, switch color scheme for 2½". At the next 7mm gold bead, switch color scheme back. Make the strap 39" long and secure at opposite corner of pouch.

Porcupine Heart Pattern

Porcupine Heart Fringe

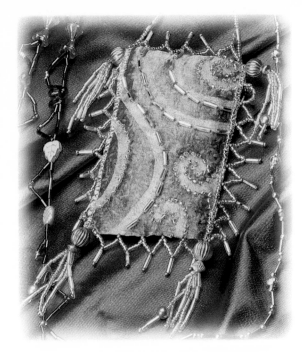

Copper Ribbon Sachet

MATERIALS: 9" of 2½" ribbon
BEADS: 11/0 champagne silver lined seed • 11/0 copper opaque seed • Champagne silver lined bugle • Four 10mm copper • Assorted decorative copper
INSTRUCTIONS: Mark center panel for front. Stitch beads along design on ribbon. Turn under both short ends and press. Fold each end to center and overlap ½" at back. Whip stitch long edges closed.

Fill and close sachet.

Start at a corner and work bead fringe around all 4 sides. Anchor the thread and string copper seed, 5 champagne seed, copper seed, bugle and copper seed

Pass needle back through bugle and second copper seed. Add 5 more champagne and a copper seed. Stitch to sachet edge about ⅜" from anchor. Go back through the stitched copper bead and repeat the pattern starting with 5 champagne seeds. Fringe around all 4 edges.

At each corner, make a tassel with a 10mm round copper bead base and several strands of champagne seed and bugle beads. Add decorative copper beads at random.

Add a beaded chain by alternating 5 seed beads with one bugle to desired length, anchor at corners.

Copper Fringe

Grapes Pouch

MATERIALS: 8" of 2½" maroon satin ribbon with gold edging • 45" of Soft Touch™ .010 diameter wire • Velvet grape leaf removed from a silk flower or plant • Beading thread and needle • Sewing thread and needle
BEADS: 11/0 grape purple silver lined seed • 11/0 dusty purple silver lined seed • 11/0 metallic lavender seed • 6/0 purple color inside seed • 10/0 metallic purple/bronze variegated seed • Short silver lined grape purple • Gold and mauve bugle
DECORATIVE BEADS: Glass grape cluster • Frosted green glass leaf • Oblong purple rectangle • Grape teardrop • Green/purple twist • Purple gold engraved round • Round red iridescent • Oversized iridescent red bugle • Lavender pineapple • Purple faceted disk • Purple blossom shape • 6/0 frosted purple rochaille • Small frosted purple teardrop
INSTRUCTIONS: Fold ribbon in half. Fold under ¼" at top of each panel, and fold under ¼" again. Whip stitch to finish edges.

Tack grape leaf with carefully removed stem wire to front of pouch. Stitch grape purple seeds to form a cluster shape. Stitch additional layers of beads on the base layer making each layer narrower than the previous one. End with 3 or 4 layers of beads which resemble a dimensional cluster of grapes.

Twist ends of the stem wire you removed from the leaf into tendrils and bend in half. Stitch to leaf above grape cluster.

Stitch gold bugle beads across the top edge of the pouch front.

Work bead fringe along the bottom of the front. Start at center and make the longest strand. Work to one side decreasing the lengths of strands. Duplicate the pattern on the opposite side.

Add a bead swag in front of the fringe using dusty purple seeds with 6/0 and decorative beads.

Whip stitch the sides of the pouch to close.

Strap - Secure wire at top corner of pouch. Work first strand by alternating decorative beads between ¾" lengths of short purple bugles. At 19½", the center point, reverse the pattern and continue until strap is 39" long. Secure at opposite corner of pouch.

Thread beading needle with beading thread and make second strand by passing through the decorative beads of the first strand and stringing about 1" of bugles and seeds in between. The extra lengths of beads will form loops when you pass the thread back through the decorative beads from the first strand.

Use beading thread to create bead tassels at the corners where the strap is attached.

Grape Fringe Swag

Cameo Pouch

MATERIALS: Scraps of ribbons and fabrics • Flat cotton batting • Lacis gold purse frame #LS 69 • Kreinik #8 black, fuchsia and blue braid • Creative Beginnings gold charm frame #4820 • Copy of photo sized to fit in frame • 39" gold chain for strap

BEADS: 11/0 neon purple inside color seed • 11/0 black shadow opaque luster seed • 8/0 paradise blue inside rainbow seed • 8mm purple glass wafers • 11/0 metallic copper seed

INSTRUCTIONS: Cut one pattern piece from batting and 2 from fabric. One will be the lining for the patchwork piece. Arrange scraps of ribbons and fabrics on the batting. Turn under raw edges and pin in place. Embroider over seams leaving seam allowance around edges free of stitching. Add bead embellishments at ends of embroidery stitches.

Trim copy of photo to fit in frame. Position frame in center of patchwork and adjust slightly toward bottom so frame is about ¾" above seam allowance. Carefully use a sharp blade to make 4 tiny punctures in the patchwork to insert the frame tabs. Bend tabs snugly to back of batting. Baste lining to wrong side of patchwork below dots.

With right sides together, stitch front to back below dots. Clip curves and turn right side out. Turn top edge of back over ¼" twice and hem. Turn top edge of patchwork and lining to inside and stitch to cover raw edges.

Run a gathering stitch along the top edges of the pouch. Adjust to fit and stitch to purse frame.

Make a beaded loop fringe along the frame with individual loops of 7 purple, copper, 20 purple, copper and 7 purple beads. Skip 3 holes and stitch to frame. Backtrack to hole on the right of the first loop and make a second loop. Repeat to cover all the holes in the frame with loops.

Make a bead fringe around the bottom of the pouch by starting in center and stringing on black, purple, copper, more purple and black seeds. Add a wafer and end with a black seed to anchor. Return thread through all the other beads and stitch to fabric. Bring thread out of fabric ¼" away. Add another strand of beads decreasing the number of seeds. Continue working away from center decreasing beads with each strand. When you get to the end of one side, repeat the same pattern from the center strand in the other direction.

Finish pouch by attaching 39" chain to the purse frame.

Cameo Purse Pattern

Fold

Charmed Heart Sachet

MATERIALS: 4" square of magenta organza • 7/0 pink silver lined seed beads • 11/0 snowflake Ceylon seed beads • Assorted heart charms, buttons and decorative beads

INSTRUCTIONS: Fold organza square in half to make a triangle. Sew around raw edges leaving a small opening to turn right side out. Make a gathering stitch along the fold.

Fill and close sachet. Pull up gathers along fold and form into a heart shape. Stitch ends in place.

For hanger loop, anchor beading thread at center top and string 2 pink beads and 3" of white beads. Return needle through pink beads and anchor to fabric.

Bead Fringe - Come back up through fabric next to the loop and string on 10 white beads, pink bead and 10 white beads. Anchor to fabric about ½" from first bead. Return needle through last 2 white beads and add 8 more whites, pink and 10 whites. Anchor ½" away. Repeat around the entire edge of the heart.

Stitch charms, buttons and beads on front of sachet.

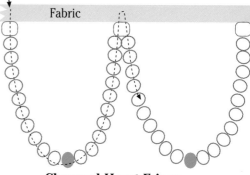

Fabric

Charmed Heart Fringe

Reversible Girl & Spool Vintage Advertising Pouch

MATERIALS: 5" x 7" piece of white satin and pale blue satin • 2 vintage images or other images sized to 2½" x 3¾" • 45" piece of Soft Touch™ .010 diameter wire • Beading thread and needle • Sewing thread and needle

BEADS: 8/0 metallic silver seed • 11/0 violet spark silver lined seed • 11/0 black shadow opaque luster • 11/0 neon green inside color • 8/0 paradise blue inside rainbow seed bead • 1" amethyst silver lined bugle • Size 5 rainbow mauve silver lined bugle • 2 packages of assorted amethyst glass decorative

INSTRUCTIONS: For bead borders, stitch every 2 beads to fabric.

Girl/Flower Image - Alternate 2 neon green with 2 violet sparks around image.

Spool Image - Stitch a double border using black shadow seeds for the inner row and 8/0 blues for the outer row.

Fold under ¼" at top of each panel and fold under ¼" again. Whip stitch to finish tops. With right sides together, stitch sides and bottom with ½" seam allowance.

Stitch alternating mauve bugles and metallic silver seeds around sides and bottom. Use 1" bugles, mauve bugles, silver metallic and violet spark seeds to make the fringe at bottom. At end of center strand, string decorative amethyst beads.

Strap - Secure wire at top corner of pouch. String silver metallic seed, mauve bugle, silver seed, 1" bugle, silver seed and repeat until strap is 39" long. Secure at opposite corner of pouch. Use beading thread to create bead tassels at the corners where the strap is attached.

Vintage advertising cards are highly collectible. Transfer the image to fabric using one of the methods described under basic instructions.

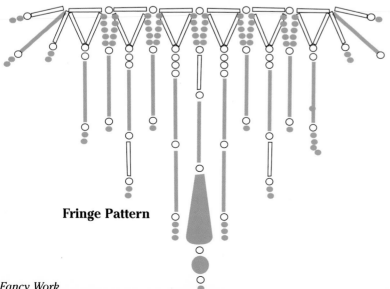

Fringe Pattern

Designs reproduced from trade card advertisements circa 1880 Coats & Clark, Inc.
from the collection of Betty Auth

Candle Holder

MATERIALS: Small blue glass candle holder with glass shade • Beading thread and needle • Beading wire

BEADS: Frosted chartreuse, variegated strands of frosted green, turquoise and blue and variegated strands of silver lined green, turquoise and blue 11/0 seed beads • Small green and turquoise frosted ovals

INSTRUCTIONS: **Candle base** - Round 1: Thread needle with 36" of thread. String 55 frosted chartreuse or enough to reach around neck using a number divisible by five. Knot securely around neck leaving a 3" tail.

Round 2: String 14 frosted chartreuse, turquoise oval, 12 frosted chartreuse, turquoise oval and frosted chartreuse. Go back through turquoise oval, 12 seed beads, and first turquoise oval. Add 14 frosted chartreuse. Pass needle through the 12th bead in Round 1. Repeat 4 more times around base ending where Round 2 started.

Round 3: Add 5 variegated frosted seed, green oval, 11 frosted chartreuse, green oval and 11 frosted chartreuse. Pass needle back through first oval and variegated beads. Pass needle through 11 beads in Round 1 and repeat 4 times around base. Tie thread ends in knot and thread the needle back through several beads before cutting.

Candle Shade - Round 1: String 84 frosted chartreuse on beading wire. Pull wire snug and knot to

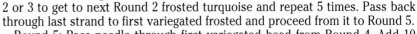

Round 1
Start Round 2
Start Round 3

Start Round 4
Silver Lined Seed
Start Round 5
Start Round 6
Start Round 7
Start Round 8
Chartreuse Frosted
Start Round 9
9th Silver Lined Bead Round 9
30th Silver Lined Bead Round 9
Start Round 10
Start Round 11
This is bottom bead of Round 4

Candle Holder Shade Fringe Pattern

secure before cutting. Thread needle with 36" of beading thread and pass through several beads in ring to secure.

Round 2: Emerge from ring and add frosted turquoise bead from variegated beads, 15 frosted chartreuse and pass needle back through the 15th bead of Round 1. Repeat 5 times ending at the starting point.

Round 3: Pass needle through turquoise bead from Round 2, add 17 frosted chartreuse, pass needle through next Round 2 frosted turquoise bead and repeat, around.

Round 4: Pass needle through first frosted turquoise bead from Round 2, add 10 frosted chartreuse and 1 variegated frosted 4 times; add 10 frosted chartreuse, turquoise oval and silver lined seed. Pass needle back through turquoise oval and up through entire strand. Pass through Rounds 1, 2 or 3 to get to next Round 2 frosted turquoise and repeat 5 times. Pass back through last strand to first variegated frosted and proceed from it to Round 5.

Round 5: Pass needle through first variegated bead from Round 4. Add 10 variegated frosted, silver lined seed, 10 variegated frosted, pass through next Round 4 variegated frosted and repeat.

Round 6: Pass through beads to second Round 4 variegated bead, add 12 variegated frosted, pass through round 5 silver lined bead, add 12 variegated frosted, pass through next Round 4 variegated bead. Repeat.

Round 7: Pass needle back through Round 6 starting bead and add 14 frosted chartreuse, turquoise oval, 14 frosted chartreuse and pass needle through next Round 4 position 2 variegated bead. Repeat.

Round 8: Pass needle to third variegated bead in round 4. Add 16 variegated silver lined, frosted chartreuse, 16 variegated silver lined, pass through next round 4 bead and repeat.

Round 9: Pass needle to fourth round 4 variegated bead. Add 19 variegated silver lined, pass through Round 8 frosted chartreuse, add 10 frosted chartreuse, green oval, 10 frosted chartreuse, turquoise oval and silver lined seed. Pass back through all beads just strung to round 8 frosted chartreuse. Pass through that bead, add 19 variegated silver lined beads and pass through next position 4 Round 4 bead. Repeat.

Round 10: From the seed bead just above the Round 4 green oval, add 10 frosted chartreuse, pass through 9th silver lined Round 9 bead, add 10 frosted chartreuse, pass through the bead above Round 9 green oval, add 10 frosted chartreuse, pass through 30th silver lined Round 9 bead, add 10 frosted chartreuse, pass through next Round 4 strand just above the green oval. Repeat.

Round 11: Add swags of 9 frosted chartreuse, turquoise oval and 9 frosted chartreuse between ovals in Rounds 4 and 9.

Pass needle back through beads to get to starting knot and pull thread snug. Tie a final knot and thread the needle back through several beads before cutting.

Base Fringe Pattern

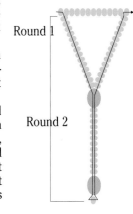

Round 1
Round 2

Round 3

Beaded Bottles & Jars

Blue Bottle

MATERIALS: 5" tall bottle with cork • Beading thread and needle • ½" and ¾" sequin pins • 1" dress pin with silver ball head • Craft stick

BEADS: 11/0 aquamarine silver lined seed • Size 2 silver lined bugle • 11/0 copen transparent frost seed • 8/0 golden plum inside rainbow • Aquamarine glass assortment

INSTRUCTIONS: Round 1: Thread needle with 36" of thread. String on five 11/0 aquamarine seed, 8/0 plum and repeat six times. Knot securely around neck of bottle leaving a 3" tail.

Round 2: Pass needle through a plum bead, add five 11/0 copen, silver bugle, 8/0 plum, silver bugle, five 11/0 copen and pass needle through next Round 1 plum. Repeat.

Round 3: Pass needle through Round 2 plum. Add silver bugle, four 11/0 aquamarine, plum, large aquamarine bugle from glass assortment, plum, 6mm round aquamarine, 11/0 aquamarine seed. Pass needle back through 6mm aquamarine and rest of beads back to first Round 3 plum. Add silver bugle, four 11/0 aquamarine. Pass through next Round 2 plum and repeat. Pass needle back through beads to starting knot and pull thread snug. Tie a final knot and thread the needle back through several beads before cutting.

Cork - For the swag, string 4 repetitions of silver bugle, three copen, silver bugle, three copen, silver bugle, 5mm aquamarine, silver bugle, three copen, bugle, three copen, silver bugle. Tie ends together and secure knot. Cut tails. Set aside. Select 8 bean shape beads from the assortment. Using ½" sequin pins, slide on aquamarine seed, plum seed and a bean shape bead. One by one, pin to the edge of the cork using craft stick to gently push in.

Between each bean bead pin, place another pin with a single seed bead part way into the cork. Drape the swag from these, and push the pins into the cork as far as they will go.

Add beads from the assortment to the dress pin, leaving at least ⅜" to stick into the center of cork.

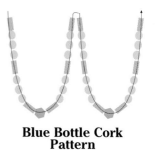

Blue Bottle Fringe Pattern

Blue Bottle Cork Pattern

Round 2

Round 3

TIP: *Purchase pre-strung hanks of beads for faster beading. While the beads are still on the strings, you can place them on a bead tray and slide needle and thread into the strand and pull off several beads at once.*

Magenta Bottle

MATERIALS: 4½" tall bottle with cork • Beading thread and needle • ½" and ¾" sequin pins • 1" hat pin with pearl • Craft stick

BEADS: 11/0 violet spark silver lined seed • 12 crystal iris bugle • Size 5 mauve silver lined mauve bugle • 8/0 violet blue inside rainbow seed • 13 aquamarine iridescent glass hearts

INSTRUCTIONS: Round 1: On 36" of beading thread, alternate six violet, one violet blue and repeat enough times to go around neck of bottle. Knot securely around neck leaving a 3" tail.

Round 2: Bring needle out through violet, add six violet, pass back through Round 1 violet 3 beads over from start of Round 2. This makes a little loop. Repeat to make a bead ruffle around the bottle.

Round 3: Bring needle out of Round 1 violet blue, add 7 violet, 3 violet blue, heart, violet blue and violet. Return through violet blue, heart and 3 violet blue. Add 7 violet and pass through next violet blue Round 1 bead. Add 13 violet, violet blue, violet, violet blue, violet, violet blue, bugle, violet blue, heart, violet blue, violet, violet blue and violet. Return through entire strand to Round 1 violet blue, pass through and repeat sequence. Pass needle back through beads to starting knot and pull thread snug. Tie a final knot and thread the needle back through several beads before cutting.

Cork - Use ½" sequin pins with violet blue beads to form outer rim. Alternate pins with 3, 2, 1, 2 and 3 violet blue beads each topped with violet seed. Use the craft stick to push the pins all the way into the cork. Use ¾" pins with violet, blue violet and a mauve bugle for inner tier.

On the hat pin, put blue violet, heart, blue violet and bugle and place in center of cork.

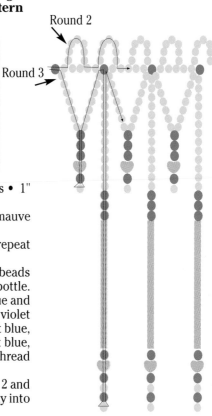

Round 2

Round 3

Magenta Bottle Fringe Pattern

Potpourri Dish

MATERIALS: 5" covered potpourri dish •
Beading thread and needle

BEADS: 11/0 American blue opaque seed • 11/0
forget-me-not Ceylon seed • 8/0 paradise blue
inside rainbow seed • 8mm blue glass wafers •
Size 5 cobalt blue silver lined bugle • Cobalt
blue with gold imprint triangle shape decorative • Small frosted blue oval

INSTRUCTIONS: Round 1: Thread needle with
36" of thread. String 5 11/0 frosted blue ovals
and Ceylon seed. Repeat around neck of dish.
Knot securely around neck of jar leaving a 3"
tail.

Round 2: Bring needle out at Round 1 ceylon,
add 5 ceylon seeds, blue oval, 5 ceylon seeds
and pass through next Round 1 ceylon. Repeat
around Round 1.

Round 3: Bring needle out through Round 2
oval, add 3 paradise blue seed, blue wafer and 3
paradise blue seed. Pass through next Round 2
oval and repeat around Round 2.

Round 4: Bring needle out through Round 3
wafer, add 5 ceylon seed, paradise blue seed
and 5 ceylon seed. Pass through next Round 3 wafer and repeat around Round 3.

Round 5: Bring needle out through Round 4 paradise blue seed, add 3 frosted blue seed, paradise blue seed, bugle, oval and frosted blue seed. Pass back through oval, bugle and paradise
blue seed. Add 3 frosted blue seed and pass through next Round 4 paradise blue seed. Add 3
frosted blue seed, triangle bead and 3 frosted blue seed. Pass through next Round 4 paradise
blue seed. Repeat around Round 4.

Pass needle back to starting point in Round 1, tie thread ends in knot and thread the needle
back through several beads before cutting.

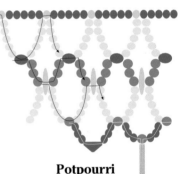

**Potpourri
Dish Fringe**

Pomander Jar

MATERIALS: Floral Mist Gazebo Scents Gel Pomander Jar by Carolina Designs • Beading thread
and needle

BEADS: 11/0 dusty purple silver lined seed • 8/0 blue fuchsia lined seed • 6/0 purple silver lined
seed • Short grape purple silver lined bugle • 1" opaque orchid bugle

INSTRUCTIONS: Round 1: Thread needle with 36" of thread. String on enough grape bugles to
reach around neck of bottle using a number of beads divisible by 6. Knot securely around neck
of jar leaving a 3" tail.

Round 2: Pass needle through a bugle, string on 4 grape bugles, 2 blue seed, 1" orchid
bugle and dusty purple seed. Pass back through 1" bugle and blue seeds, add 4
grape bugles. Count 5 bugles in Round 1 from where thread emerged to begin
Round 2 and pass needle back through the next bugle in Round 1. Bring needle
out and repeat around bottle.

Round 3: Pass needle through 4 grape bugles and first blue seed from Round
2, string alternating grape bugle, blue seed, grape bugle, blue seed, grape bugle,
2 purple seed, blue seed, purple seed; pass needle back through glue seed and
2 purple seed. Add grape bugle, blue seed, grape bugle, blue seed, grape
bugle. Pass back through next Round 2 blue seed. Repeat sequence for
Round 3 around entire jar. Pass needle back through beads to starting knot
and pull thread snug. Tie a final knot and thread the needle back through
several beads before cutting.

Round 3

Rounds
1 & 2

**Pomander
Jar
Fringe**

Hexagonal Doily

MATERIALS: 4" hexagonal crocheted doily • Organza cut 1" larger than doily on all sides • Satin for backing • Fancy button

BEADS: 11/0 magenta silver lined seed • 11/0 chartreuse silver lined seed • 12/0 pink color inside seed • 8/0 pink Ceylon • Mauve bugle

INSTRUCTIONS: Center and baste doily to organza. Stitch a sequence of magenta seed, chartreuse seed and magenta seed around the outer edges of doily at 6 points.

Stitch 6 mini tassels to doily as follows: Come up and string one pink Ceylon, 5 magenta seed and chartreuse seed.

Pass needle back through magenta and ceylon beads to complete the first tendril. Take a stitch at the back of the fabric. Come back up through the pink Ceylon and repeat to make 3 more tendrils. Anchor to fabric and proceed to next tassel.

Sew backing pieces to sachet top using a ¼" seam allowance.

Start bead edging at one of the 6 points.

Round 1: Anchor thread and add one pink Ceylon, bugle and pink seed. Pass needle back through bugle and Ceylon. Stitch to fabric and come back out through the pink Ceylon. Add 6 magenta seed, chartreuse seed, 6 magenta seed and pink Ceylon. Stitch to fabric approximately ½" from anchor. Come back up through the large pink, add bugle and pink seed. Loop around, return through bugle and pink Ceylon and stitch. Come back up through pink Ceylon and repeat around edge of the sachet.

Round 2: At starting point, take needle back through the pink Ceylon, first 6 magenta seed and chartreuse seed. Add 6 magenta seed, chartreuse seed, 6 magenta seed and back through the next existing chartreuse seed. Repeat around edge.

Fill and close sachet.

Blind anchor beading thread in the edge seam and come up through top layer of organza ½" directly above a bugle bead stack. Catch the chartreuse bead from Round 2 and stitch to fabric above the bugle stack flipping the bead fringe on the sachet top. Run the thread behind the sachet top to the next point and stitch the next chartreuse bead in place. The sachet filling should hide the thread. Stitch each chartreuse bead in place around the sachet.

Sew fancy button to the center of the top.

Round Doily

MATERIALS: 5" round crocheted doily pre-dyed in mauves • 6" circle of organza • Satin for back • HeatnBond Lite iron-on adhesive • 2" off-white crocheted flower

BEADS: Lavender, purple, purple silver lined and pink metallic 11/0 seed • 10/0 pink parfait silky cut seed • 11/0 flamingo silver lined seed • 10 pendant or drop beads as dictated by doily • 3 decorative beads for center stack

INSTRUCTIONS: Stitch ½" seam allowance around organza circle. Clip for ease and press under along stitching. Use the iron-on adhesive to fuse the doily to the top of the organza.

Center the crocheted flower on the doily and baste in place. Stitch individual seed beads to the doily and flower following the crocheted rows and patterns.

Turn under outer edges of backing and hand sew to top leaving edges of doily hanging free. Stitch pendant beads to edge of doily. Stitch a bead fringe to edge of doily by anchoring thread and stringing 5 pink seed, silky cut pink seed, 5 pink seed and stitching to edge of doily ¼" from anchor. Allow beads to drape and hang free. Continue around doily.

Fill and close sachet.

Anchor beading thread at center of back and go up through center of top. Add the 3 decorative beads with largest at bottom and finish by looping around a seed bead on top. Take thread back through beads and sachet and pull tight. Overstitch to secure.

Teacup Pincushion

MATERIALS: Teacup and saucer • 6" crocheted doily • 10" circle of blue satin • 24" of narrow blue ribbon • Beading thread and needle • Batting • Sand

BEADS: Size 5 cobalt blue silver lined bugle • 1" crystal iris bugle • Two packages of 8mm blue glass wafers • 8/0 paradise blue inside rainbow seed • 6mm iridescent black glass • 11/0 spearmint transparent rainbow seed

INSTRUCTIONS: Stitch spearmint beads around edge of doily. Stitch long dangles at 'peaks' of the scallops and short dangles in 'valleys'.

Long dangles - cobalt blue bugle, crystal iris bugle, blue wafer, 6mm black, blue seed and spearmint seed. Pass needle back through beads and stitch to doily edge.

Short dangles - blue seed, blue bugle, blue seed, blue wafer, blue seed and spearmint seed. Pass needle back through beads and stitch to doily edge.

Weave the narrow ribbon in and out of the doily about 1" from edge.

Gather the satin 1" from edge and pull up leaving an opening about 2" across. Place batting into the circle and pour in sand until about 2" from being full. Stuff in more batting and draw gathers tight. Work the filled satin shape into the teacup. It should protrude in a dome shape a few inches above the top of the cup.

Place the doily on the stuffed satin and pull up the ribbon to gather tightly at the rim of the cup. Tie in a bow.

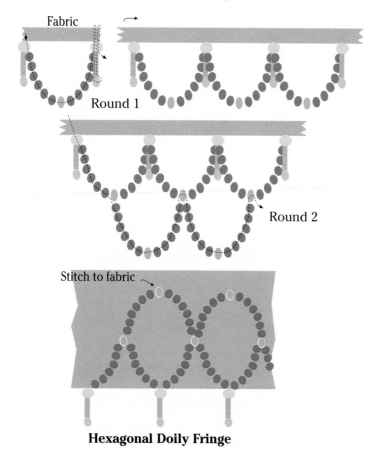

Hexagonal Doily Fringe

Basic Embroidery Stitches for Crazy Quilting

U - bring needle up   D - take needle down

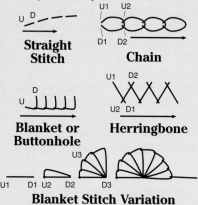

Straight Stitch   **Chain**

Blanket or Buttonhole   **Herringbone**

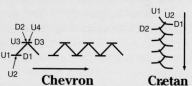

Blanket Stitch Variation

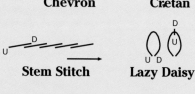

Chevron   **Cretan**

Stem Stitch   **Lazy Daisy**

Fly or Y   **Feather**

Closed Blanket Stitch
Up at 1, down at 2, up at 3, down at 4.

Couching
Stitch across separate thread or cord with small straight stitches.

Satin Stitch
Make straight stitches close together.

Maidenhair
Work graduated feather stitches.

Sheaf
Make 3 parallel stitches. Come up at center next to middle stitch. Slide needle behind left stitch, cross over and go behind the right stitch and down at center pulling outer legs toward the center.

French Knot
Bring needle up and wrap thread around it. Take needle back down close to where you came up pushing knot down as you draw the needle to pull the thread snug.

Crazy Quilting Basics

Crazy-quilting provides an opportunity to combine lots of your favorite fabrics, beads and other embellishments in one project. The only difficulty is knowing when to stop embellishing! You do not have to do a lot of planning, your project will evolve as you work.

Rather than stitch the pieces together first, pin them onto a foundation of muslin or flat batting. I highly recommend Fairfield All-Natural Cotton batting. Fold the edges of the top pieces under ¼" to ½" where they overlap. Use lots of pins! Decorative embroidery over each seam will hold the pieces together. Remove the pins as you embroider. It takes a little practice to learn how to hold the fabric so a pin is not sticking you and to keep the embroidery thread from getting caught on the pin. Embroider outer patches first and work toward the center. That way you will be dealing with fewer pins when you are in the middle of your work. If you prefer, you can hand baste the patches in place and get rid of the pins before you do the embroidery.

With a foundation of cotton batting, you will not need an embroidery hoop since the batting will maintain its shape and allow you to fold the work as needed to access the area you want to embroider. It is not necessary to stretch the fabric taut. Mark your seam allowance on the front and back of the foundation. Stay stitching will do this in one step.

As you lay out the patchwork on the foundation, pick out trims and laces and decide where you might incorporate them. Tuck the ends under the patches as you embroider and stitch right on top of the trims with small, invisible straight tacking stitches. If you decide you want to add a trim or lace later, you have the option of doing so at any time before the seam is embroidered.

Decorative embroidery holds the patches in place and gives crazy patchwork its signature look. The stitches are basic embroidery, often combined for elaborate looking borders, but all are easily accomplished. Basic stitches include Fly or Y, Feather, Cretan, Lazy Daisy, Chain, Blanket or Buttonhole, Stem, Straight, Herringbone, Chevron and French Knot, all of which have many variations. Try them all and you will soon discover your favorites. Keep stitching out of the seam allowance to avoid accidentally cutting through it during final assembly.

Patches - Use any fabric scraps you like. This is an excellent way to make use of tiny scraps you would otherwise discard. Wide fabric ribbons are perfect for patches. You may only use a 3" length so a yard will go a long way! If the ribbon happens to come with wire edges, simply pull the wire out. With most ribbons, the edges are already finished so you will not have to turn them under. If you do not have fabrics, consider making an entire piece from wide ribbon patches or purchase very small amounts of yardage. Even a ¼ yard will yield many patches!

Solid colors are most suitable because the finished piece is busy enough with all the embroidery and embellishing. Use printed fabrics sparingly, if at all, and surround printed patches with solids. Decorative stitching may not show up well on a printed patch, so this can be an ideal place to use trims to cover the seams.

Thread - One of the best tips I can give you is not to use embroidery floss. Perle cotton # 8 or #5 is much better for this kind of embroidery. Metallic thread and fine braids by Kreinik look beautiful. Rayon threads are lovely but take a little more patience to manage as they tend to tangle. A fine weight crochet or heavier tatting thread will work well, too.

Choose thread that contrasts with the background fabric so your fancy stitching will show. Use 18" to 24" lengths. Any longer and you will be fighting knots and tangles. Using quilter's beeswax to coat thread will help prevent knots but I do not recommend it for metallic threads.

Needles - Use embroidery or chenille needles with a fairly large eye, and sharp tip.

Silk Ribbons - Silk ribbon embroidery works wonderfully on crazy quilts. Embroider motifs on patches or use the ribbon to stitch embroidery that holds the seams in place. Use appropriate silk ribbon embroidery needles.

Beads and Pearls - Use a double strand of good quality beading thread or fine metallic sewing thread and the correct size beading needles. Anchor every one or two beads to hold in place and prevent them from being snagged.

Embellishments - The sky's the limit! Parts of old and new jewelry, buttons, charms, bits of crochet, lace, trims, feathers… anything you can stitch down is fair game for use in your crazy quilt. Decorative cord can be couched into place and spiraled for wonderful effect. The hard part is knowing when you are finished because as you go, you will have so many ideas for things you would like to try.

Books - There are many excellent books available on crazy quilting, embroidery and embellishment. Here are a few of my favorites:

Elegant Stitches by Judith Baker Montano, C&T Publishing, 1995
The Magic of Crazy Quilting by J. Marsha Michler, Krause Publications, 1998
Crazy Quilt Stitches by Dorothy Bond, 1981
Crazy Patchwork by Janet Haigh, The Quilt Digest Press, 1998
Victorian Elegance by Lezette Thomason, That Patchwork Place, 1996
Crazy Patchwork by Meryl Potter, The Lothian Craft Series, 1997
Crazy Quilting by Christine Dabbs, Rutledge Hill Press, 1998
An Encyclopedia of Crazy Quilt Stitches by Linda Causee, American School of Needlework, 1997.

Crazy Quilt Stocking

MATERIALS: Stocking pattern of choice • Photocopy that has been reversed and transfer medium of your choice • Scraps of fabric or wide ribbon in greens and burgundies • 12" x 36" piece of Fairfield All-Natural cotton batting • 24" x 36" piece of fabric for lining • 12" x 36" piece of fabric for backing • Short pieces of fancy trims • One large and one small tassel • #8 perle and Kreinik metallic embroidery threads • 1/8" or narrower braid ribbon for some embroidery • One yard of fine gold braid for cuff design • Seed and bugle beads • 24 gold 1/4" jingle bells • Larger fancy beads • Charms • Buttons and bells • Embroidery and chenille needles • Beading needle

INSTRUCTIONS: Create the body of the stocking following the pattern and basic crazy-quilting instructions.

Cuff - Cut one batting and one backing piece. Stay stitch or otherwise mark the seam allowances. Pin or baste fabric on cuff. Couch gold braid, looped along each seam. Trim batting from seam allowances avoiding any embroidery stitching or knots.

Sew backing to the cuff along bottom edge. Clip corners and turn right side out. Baste cuff to stocking at sides and top.

Finish – Trim batting from seam allowances of stocking. Pin or baste toe tassel in place on outside front. Sew backing piece to stocking along sides and bottom. Trim seams and clip curves. Turn right side out.

Cut 2 lining pieces and stitch sides and bottoms leaving a 6" or larger opening along the right long edge. Trim seams and clip curves. Do not turn.

Insert the stocking into the lining and stitch together around the top. Turn through opening in lining. Whip stitch lining closed before inserting it into stocking.

Hand sew large tassel to the top edge of the cuff and use the loop to hang the stocking.

Make beaded tassels as instructed on page 3 at the points on the cuff. Add bells on beaded loops at the bottoms of the braided seams. Further embellish the toe and hanger loop tassels by stitching beads, bells and charms to them.

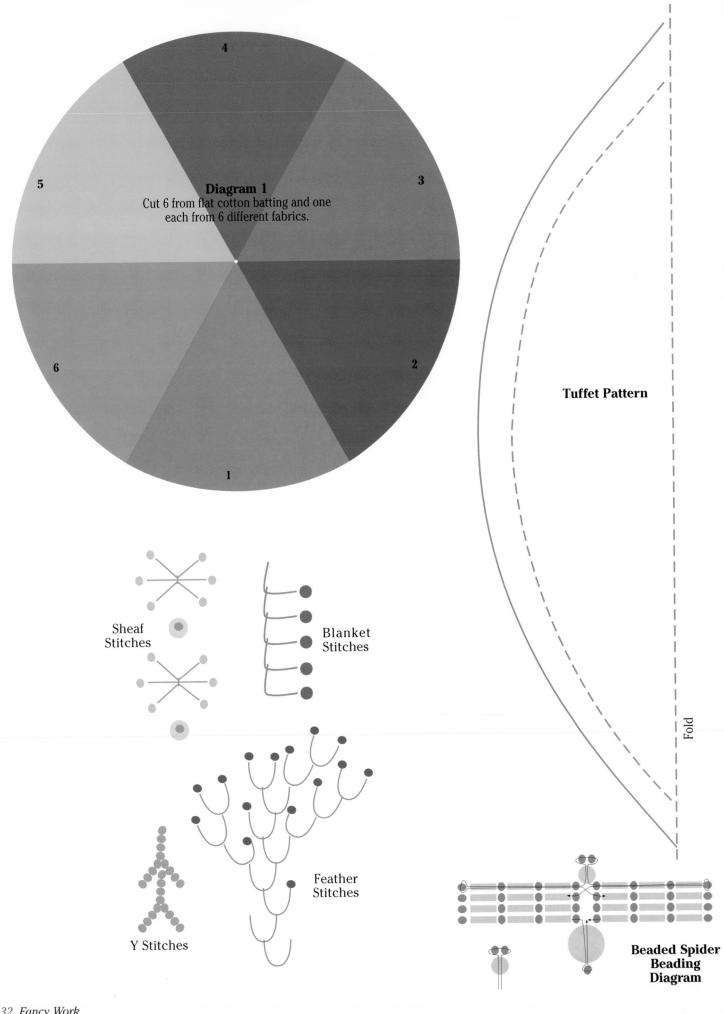

Diagram 1
Cut 6 from flat cotton batting and one
each from 6 different fabrics.

4

5

3

6

2

1

Tuffet Pattern

Fold

Sheaf
Stitches

Blanket
Stitches

Feather
Stitches

Y Stitches

**Beaded Spider
Beading
Diagram**

Miss Muffet Cushion

MATERIALS: 5" x 9" pieces of velvet in 6 colors - burgundy (4), green (6) and purple (2) velvet, magenta (3), purple (1) and chartreuse (5) brocade • The number in ( ) indicates placement in Diagram 1 • Flat cotton batting • Fine sand • Hi-loft batting • Kreinik #1 and #5 Japan silver thread • Kreinik #8 purple braid • Kreinik Facets red cord • Dark red sewing thread • Purple and green pearl cotton embroidery thread • 2 large flat buttons • Rug thread • Long, heavy-duty needle • Oatmeal box for base • Purple fabric to cover box • Wright's 3" purple bullion fringe • PeelnStick double-sided adhesive

BEADS: 11/0 and 7/0 clear silver lined • 11/0 metallic pink • 11/0 and 9/0 burgundy • 11/0 purple • 11/0 light green • 7mm peach pearls

SPIDER MATERIALS: 24 blue ½" bugle beads • 35 blue 11/0 seed beads • 6mm round blue bead for head • 15mm blue berry bead for body • Beading wire

INSTRUCTIONS: Cut 6 pattern pieces from batting and one from each of the 6 fabric colors. Refer to diagram 1 for fabric placement. With a fabric piece on top of a batting piece, machine stitch pieces 6, 1 and 2 together along seam lines. Stitch 3, 4 and 5 together so you have 2 separate halves of the pincushion. Embellish the seams as follows:

Seams 1-2 and 4-5: Sheaf stitches with green or purple pearl thread. Sew a seed at the end of each stitch, green seeds with green thread and magenta seeds with purple thread. Between each sheaf, stitch a peach pearl and green seed.

Seams 6-1 and 3-4: With beading thread and metallic pink beads, make Y stitches using 8 beads for the top of each Y and 4 beads for stem.

On the purple brocade panel, couch #5 silver thread with #1 silver thread to form a spider web design.

On the purple velvet panel, make a dragonfly following pattern and instructions provided in the sachet section on page 5.

Couch red cord in a meandering pattern across magenta and burgundy panels.

Hand or machine stitch halves together between panels 5 & 6. Work a feather-stitch pattern with #8 purple braid and purple seeds.

Stitch remaining panels together ⅔ of the way and work blanket stitches over the seam with purple #8 braid and burgundy seeds.

Fill ball about halfway with hi-loft batting. Add fine sand to fill rest of the way. Cover sand with a layer of batting and finish with a disk of flat batting. Hand stitch remaining seam closed.

Cut 30" of rug thread and double it in the heavy-duty needle. Pass through a button at bottom and up through center of pincushion and another button on top, back through pincushion and button at bottom. Pull threads tight and tie off.

Cut oatmeal box down to 3" and cover with purple fabric

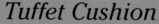

Tuffet Cushion
This spectacular tuffet pin cushion will grace any table or sewing area with its beautiful fabrics, elegant stitches and charming critters. Embellish seams and sections with lively stitches created with metallic threads and beautiful beads.

using double-sided adhesive. Wrap over top edge and into box. Attach fringe around top edge of box. Rest the tuffet on top of this base.

Spider - Start with 36" of beading wire. Take one end through smaller round bead, 2 seed, and back through round bead. Slide beads to center of wire. To one of the wire tails, alternately add seed, bugle, seed, bugle, seed, bugle and seed. Go back through bugles and seeds. Repeat for each leg. Make 4 legs, cross over wires for each new leg. When all legs are finished, take one of the tails through the blue berry bead and a seed, and back through the berry bead. Twist the 2 wire tails together tightly and cut off ends. Bend the legs to form a realistic looking spider. With beading thread, stitch spider to top of pincushion through the seed beads at the ends of the legs.

Crazy Bolster Pillow

MATERIALS: Photocopies that have been reversed and transfer medium of your choice • Bolster pillow form • Scraps of fabric or wide ribbon in greens • Fairfield All-Natural cotton batting, enough to wrap around pillow form with ½" seam allowances added to all sides plus circles for the ends • Fancy trims, ribbons and crocheted doilies • #8 perle cotton and Kreinik metallic embroidery thread • Seed and bugle beads • Larger fancy beads, charms and buttons • Embroidery and chenille needles • Beading needle

INSTRUCTIONS: Measure pillow form and make proper size pillow cover from batting following basic crazy quilting instructions. When pinning the patches, start with the photo patches and arrange the other patches around them. Make circular patchwork pieces to fit ends of pillow.

To finish, sew long edges with right sides together leaving an 8" to 10" opening in the center. Fit and stitch the end pieces in place and turn right side out.

Insert the pillow form and whip stitch the opening closed. Cover seam with fancy embroidery, if desired.